Specific Skill Series
for Reading

Drawing
Conclusions

Sixth Edition

Columbus, OH

The **McGraw·Hill** Companies

Cover: © Photodisc/Getty Images, Inc.

SRAonline.com

 SRA

Send all inquiries to:
SRA/McGraw-Hill
4400 Easton Commons
Columbus, OH 43219

ISBN 0-07-604016-X

3 4 5 6 7 8 9 BCH 12 11 10 09 08 07

TO THE TEACHER

PURPOSE:

DRAWING CONCLUSIONS helps develop one of the most important interpretive skills. Students learn to look beyond the writer's literal statements to reach an unstated but logical conclusion based on those statements and sometimes their phrasing. In **DRAWING CONCLUSIONS** the correct conclusion is the most logical one for students to reach from only the information presented.

FOR WHOM:

The skill of **DRAWING CONCLUSIONS** is developed through a series of books spanning ten levels (Picture, Preparatory, A, B, C, D, E, F, G, H). The Picture Level is for students who have not acquired a basic sight vocabulary. The Preparatory Level is for students who have a basic sight vocabulary but are not yet ready for the first-grade-level book. Books A through H are appropriate for students who can read on levels one through eight, respectively.

THE NEW EDITION:

The sixth edition of the *Specific Skill Series for Reading* maintains the quality and focus that has distinguished this program for more than 40 years. A key element central to the program's success has been the unique nature of the reading selections. Fiction and nonfiction pieces about current topics have been designed to stimulate the interest of students, motivating them to use the comprehension strategies they have learned to further their reading. To keep this important aspect of the program intact, a percentage of the reading selections has been replaced in order to ensure the continued relevance of the subject material.

In addition, a significant percentage of the artwork in the program has been replaced to give the books a contemporary look. The cover photographs are designed to appeal to readers of all ages.

SESSIONS:

Short practice sessions are the most effective. It is desirable to have a practice session every day or every other day, using a few units each session.

SCORING:

Students should record their answers on the reproducible worksheets. The worksheets make scoring easier and provide uniform records of the students' work. Using worksheets also avoids consuming the exercise books.

It is important for students to know how well they are doing. For this reason, units should be scored as soon as they have been completed. Then a discussion can be held in which students justify their choices. (The *Language Activity Pages,* many of which are open-ended, do not lend themselves to an objective score; thus there are no answer keys for these pages.)

GENERAL INFORMATION ON *DRAWING CONCLUSIONS:*

The questions in **DRAWING CONCLUSIONS** do not deal with direct references; thus the answers do not use the same words as the paragraphs. In the Picture Level, the students examine the picture for the correct answer. The Preparatory, A, and B levels contain primarily indirect references; that is, the answers are found in the paragraphs but with slightly different wording. Some easy conclusions are also included. As the books become more challenging, more difficult conclusions must be drawn, involving less obvious relationships. The conclusions also become more dependent on qualifying words such as *mostly, all, some,* or *only.*

In **DRAWING CONCLUSIONS** the readers are asked to find an example, note a contrast, generalize, see cause and effect relationships, detect a mood, see an analogy, identify a time or place relationship, make a comparison, or anticipate an outcome.

It is important that the teacher ask students to find in the paragraph the specific information relevant to the tentative conclusion. Then students must test the conclusion against the information provided. When the emphasis is placed on finding evidence to prove answers and when the students put themselves in roles of detectives, not only does their ability to draw conclusions rapidly improve, but they also have fun.

Students must know that a conclusion is a judgment made. It must be supported by strong evidence. In **DRAWING CONCLUSIONS** the correct answer is one that is either highly likely or certain.

Some alternate answer choices may be true. The answer that is accepted as correct, however, must not only be true but must also have supportive evidence in the paragraph. The clue may hinge on a single word, involve a phrase or a sentence, or encompass the paragraph as a whole.

RELATED MATERIALS:

Specific Skill Series Assessment Book provides the teacher with a pretest and a posttest for each skill at each grade level. These tests will help the teacher assess the students' performance in each of the nine comprehension skills.

A writer does not tell you everything in a story. Sometimes you need to figure out things on your own. This is called **drawing a conclusion.** A conclusion is what you can tell from what the writer tells you.

Good readers draw conclusions as they read. They use what the writer tells them. Drawing a conclusion is like answering a riddle. Read this riddle. Think about the clues it gives. Can you tell what this thing is?

I have a face and hands. I often hang on a wall. I can tell you the time of day.

Did you guess that this is a clock? You can draw that conclusion from clues in the riddle.

In this book, you will read stories. For each story, choose the answer that tells what you can conclude from the story. Remember to use clues in the story to draw a conclusion.

Fish make good pets. They need clean water and something to eat. Fish swim up and down and around. They never stop. It is fun to see them eat and play.

From the story you can tell that

    (A) pet fish are often blue.

    (B) people eat with their pet fish.

    (C) fish keep moving.

Our car is lost. Where can it be? We look and look. We cannot find our new red car. There it is. It is on the other side of that big blue bus.

From the story you can tell that

    (A) a big bus can hide a car.

    (B) the bus took the car's place.

    (C) red cars can go fast.

Zack and his mom went to the park. Soon it began to rain. "Oh, no!" said Zack. "We are going to get wet!"

"It is all right," said Zack's mom. "I brought an umbrella."

From the story you can tell that

    (A) Zack's mom knew it might rain.

    (B) Zack's mom was surprised by the rain.

    (C) Zack and his mom like snow.

The cat was after the bird. Then another bird came to help its friend. Soon another bird came. Now they were all after the cat. The cat ran away!

From the story you can tell that
- **(A)** the cat began the fight.
- **(B)** the birds began the fight.
- **(C)** the cat did not run away.

The children had a turtle race. One turtle was in front. Then it stopped. The children began to laugh. What a surprise! The turtle had gone to sleep.

From the story you can tell that

   (A) one turtle was tired.
   (B) the children did not think that the race was funny.
   (C) turtles sleep all day.

The house behind Ann's house was on fire! Ann ran to tell her mom and dad. Soon the firefighters came. They put out the fire. "Thanks, Ann," said a firefighter. "You did the right thing."

From the story you can tell that

    (A) Ann tried to put out the fire.

    (B) Mom and Dad ran away.

    (C) Mom and Dad called the firefighters.

A cow was in the road. It would not move. Then a farmer came. The farmer took the cow away. "Thanks," said the people in the cars. "We could have been here all day!"

From the story you can tell that
> **(A)** the farmer helped the people.
> **(B)** the cow did not go away.
> **(C)** the cow got into a truck.

"Look at this!" cried Eva. "Come see what the baby has done!" Mom came to look. What had he done? Then she saw. The baby had built a tower of blocks!

From the story you can tell that

    (A) Mom likes to play with toys.

    (B) Eva saw the baby's tower first.

    (C) Eva built a tower of blocks.

Dylan went by the monkey cage. "Where did my hat go?" asked Dylan. Then his friends began to laugh. Soon Dylan began to laugh too. The monkey had his hat. The hat was on the monkey's head!

From the story you can tell that

    (A) Dylan thought the monkey was funny.

    (B) the monkey gave the hat back to Dylan.

    (C) the monkey began to eat the hat.

"Can we give something to Rusty, the cat?" asked Julia. "It is his birthday." Grandmother went to get something. Would it be a cake? She came back. She had a toy mouse! Rusty had a happy birthday.

From the story you can tell that

(A) Rusty liked toys.

(B) Julia did not have a good time.

(C) Julia got a toy too.

The children began to play catch. Then a big dog came. David and Kyle began to run. Maria did not run. "Come back," said Maria. "I know this dog. It just wants to make friends."

From the story you can tell that

    (A) Maria had seen the dog before.

    (B) David and Kyle knew the dog.

    (C) the dog did not like David and Kyle.

At the zoo the baby elephant cried each night. The other animals could not sleep. One night the zookeeper put on a night-light. It gave just a little light. The baby elephant stopped crying and went to sleep.

From the story you can tell that

(A) the zookeeper ran out of food.

(B) the other animals did not like to sleep.

(C) the baby elephant was afraid of the dark.

At the zoo the baby elephant cried each night. The other animals could not sleep. One night the zookeeper put on a night-light. It gave just a little light. The baby elephant stopped crying and went to sleep.

A. Exercising Your Skill

Read the story above. Think about what the story says. Answer these questions.

1. Where does the story take place?

2. What was the baby elephant doing?

3. Why could the other animals not sleep?

4. Why did the zookeeper put on a night-light?

5. Why did the baby elephant go to sleep at last?

B. Expanding Your Skill

Talk about the questions in Part A. Which answers were given in the story? Which answers did you have to figure out? How did you figure out the answers?

C. Exploring Language

Tell the story of the baby elephant. Say a word to fill each blank.

The baby elephant ＿＿ each night. The other elephants could not sleep because of the ＿＿. One night the ＿＿ put on a night-light. It worked! The baby elephant went right to ＿＿!

Now tell a name for the story.

D. Expressing Yourself

Do one of these things.

1. Tell a story about a baby animal. Give your story a good ending.

2. Act out the story in Part A. Work with two or more of your classmates.

3. Draw a picture about the story in Part A. Then talk about the picture you drew.

Would you like to have a pet pig? Mr. Lewis brings his pet pig to work. They are good friends. People like to stop by to see Mr. Lewis's pet.

From the story you can tell that

  (A) many people have pet pigs.

  (B) no one looks at a pet pig.

  (C) Mr. Lewis and the pig like each other.

"Do not walk in the boat," Dad said. But James began to walk. He fell into the water. Dad got him back into the boat.

"From now on, I will do as you say," said James.

From the story you can tell that

(A) James did what his dad told him.

(B) James did not do what his dad told him.

(C) James did not get back into the boat.

Bam! Bam! What were those sounds? Pans and spoons were all around. It was just the baby and his grandfather. They were having fun making noise with the pans.

From the story you can tell that

    (A) the grandfather did not like noise.

    (B) the baby was taking a nap.

    (C) the baby was playing with the pans.

Kaya saw a little rabbit. "It will make a good pet," she said. "I will catch it." She ran and ran, but she could not catch the rabbit. "Maybe I can buy a pet at the pet store," she said.

From the story you can tell that

    (A) Kaya wanted a pet.

    (B) Kaya caught the rabbit.

    (C) the rabbit was not as fast as Kaya.

The children were walking past a big tree on the farm. "Look out," cried Kia. "There are hornets here. They have made their nest in this tree." The children went to another part of the farm to play.

From the story you can tell that

    (A) the children did not want to get hurt.

    (B) the children did not know what
        hornets are.

    (C) the children were not afraid.

It is fun to paint a picture. All you need is something nice to look at. Maybe you will want to paint a picture of some rocks by the water.

From the story you can tell that

    (A) no one will paint rocks by the water.

    (B) you can paint what you like to see.

    (C) you cannot paint a picture of an animal.

"My dog's name is Spot," said Laura.

"Why?" asked Kiko.

Then Spot walked into the room. He lay down next to Laura.

"Now I see why!" said Kiko.

From the story you can tell that

    (A) Spot was a cat.

    (B) Laura does not like dogs.

    (C) Laura's dog has spots on his fur.

A fox was after a rabbit. The rabbit went down into its home. It came up behind the fox. The fox did not see it. The rabbit got away.

From the story you can tell that

    (A) the fox went into the rabbit's home.

    (B) the rabbit could not find its home.

    (C) the fox did not get the rabbit.

The children had some bread. They gave it to the ducks. The ducks were happy. The bread was good! The children were happy too. "This is fun," they said.

From the story you can tell that

    (A) the children were ready to catch the ducks.

    (B) the children had a good time.

    (C) the ducks did not eat.

A fox was after the chickens. They could not get away. Who could help them? Then along came Rags. Rags began to bark. The fox ran away.

From the story you can tell that

    (A) the chickens had a good time.

    (B) the fox did not get the chickens.

    (C) the fox ran after Rags.

It was a big fish! Could Rosa bring it in? It was a long fight, but she did it. People came to take her picture. The fish was as big as Rosa!

From the story you can tell that

    (A) Rosa had a lot of help.

    (B) people did not think much of the fish.

    (C) it was not easy to catch the fish.

We take a bird walk. We see many kinds of birds. We hear them sing. We walk near a tree where some birds live. The father and mother birds are giving their little ones something to eat.

From the story you can tell that

    (A) a bird walk shows us how birds live.

    (B) birds like to walk and talk all day.

    (C) little birds do not eat very much.

The children were walking past a big tree on the farm. "Look out," cried Kia. "There are hornets here. They have made their nest in this tree." The children went to another part of the farm to play.

A. Exercising Your Skill

Read the story. Think about what it says. Then answer the questions below.

THE CHILDREN WERE PLAYING.

Where were the children?

What did Kia say?

What did the children do?

Why did the children leave?

B. Expanding Your Skill

Talk about the story. Does the story tell you why the children went away? What clues in the story can you use to figure it out?

C. Exploring Language

Think about these stories. Answer each question.

1. Jim and Ann were sitting at the table. They were watching television. Jim looked at the clock. "Oh, no," he said. "We need to do our homework. Mom will be home from work soon. She told us what we had to do before we watched television."

Did Ann and Jim do what their mother wanted them to do?

How can you tell?

2. "Dad," Justin said. "I washed the dog. I cleaned my room. I put away the dishes. I did just what you said to do. May I go outside and play ball now?"

Did Justin do what his father wanted him to do?

How can you tell?

D. Expressing Yourself

Think about something you like to do outdoors at a certain time of year. Tell your class about it. Do not tell what time of year you are thinking of, but give clues. See if your class can tell what time of year you are thinking of.

Sam saw a baby bird in a nest. He started to pick it up. Mom stopped him. "Do not touch the baby bird," said Mom. "The mother bird is never far away. We must go before she gets back."

From the story you can tell that

(A) the baby bird is lost.

(B) Sam is lost.

(C) the mother bird will come soon.

Tyra was on a farm. She had never been away from town. "Look, Luis," said Tyra. "What a cute baby horse."

"No," said Luis, "that is my pony. We can ride it."

From the story you can tell that

    (A) Luis had never been on a farm.

    (B) Tyra had never seen a pony.

    (C) the pony had never been on a farm.

Kim was out in front. It was the last jump. Would her horse make it? There was not time to think. Up, up, and over went the horse. Kim came in first!

From the story you can tell that

    (A) there is another jump to go.

    (B) Kim was behind.

    (C) no one caught up to Kim.

Rico and Mr. Cruz went into a little house. It was way out on the ice. They began to fish. Rico got one! It was the first fish of the day. It was a big one.

From the story you can tell that

(A) the house was made of ice.

(B) Mr. Cruz was cold.

(C) Mr. Cruz did not make the first catch.

"Come see our two rabbits," said Maria.

"You do not have two rabbits anymore," said Ann. "Look in the cage!" There were six rabbits. Four of them were new baby rabbits!

From the story you can tell that

    (A) Maria did not know there were baby rabbits.

    (B) there were three new rabbits.

    (C) the new rabbits were no surprise.

Emily put the big fish into the water. She put it in with the little fish. When she came back, the little fish was gone.

"It is not good to do that," said Rosa. "I put the little fish in a different bowl so it would be safe."

From the story you can tell that

    (A) Rosa knew where the little fish went.

    (B) Emily knew a lot about fish.

    (C) the big fish did not know where the little fish went.

Chen went to get his coat. It was on the bed. He put his hand on something. Was it his coat? It was too dark to see. Then the "something" went "Bow wow!" It was Nip.

From the story you can tell that

    (A) the room was green.

    (B) the dog was under the bed.

    (C) Chen could not see very well.

The children saw a fox. "I wish our friends were here," said Oscar. "They will say that we did not see it."

"No," said Ana, "I will take a picture. Then they will know that we saw it!"

From the story you can tell that

    (A) not many people see a fox outside of the zoo.

    (B) the fox ran away.

    (C) Oscar did not see the fox.

The lights went out. No one could see. "What can we do?" asked Jan.

Mom went over to a box. She flipped a switch. The lights went on. "Now we can see," said Mom.

From the story you can tell that

    (A) Mom knew what was wrong.

    (B) the lights went off again.

    (C) Jan made the lights go on.

David found an old penny. He took it to Mr. Cole.

"It is a good thing you let me see it," said Mr. Cole. "This penny is very old. You can get a lot of money for it."

From the story you can tell that

    (A) Mr. Cole had lost the penny.

    (B) David dropped the penny.

    (C) the penny was not new.

The dog saw its own face in the water. It thought another dog was there. It began to bark. Ella began to laugh. "You funny dog," said Ella. "That is your own face!"

From the story you can tell that
- **(A)** the dog did not like the water.
- **(B)** the dog did not know who the dog in the water was.
- **(C)** the dog did not look like the dog in the water.

The duck could not fly. What would happen? Sam took it into the house. Soon it got well. One day the duck flew into the air. It went off with the other ducks. Sam was happy.

From the story you can tell that

    (A) the duck did not get well.

    (B) Sam made a house for the duck.

    (C) Sam was glad to see the duck fly.

Ramón was in bed. He saw his sister Marta. She was up. "Why are you up?" asked Ramón.

"I am going to get a glass of water," said Marta.

From the story you can tell that

    (A) Ramón could not find Marta.

    (B) Marta wanted something to drink.

    (C) Marta could not hear Ramón.

"May I have a balloon, Dad?" asked Julia.

"Yes," he said. "What color do you want?"

"Red," said Julia. Her dad gave the man some money. Julia got her red balloon!

From the story you can tell that

(A) Julia did not want a balloon.

(B) Julia did not want a red balloon.

(C) all the balloons were not red.

Emily put the big fish into the water. She put it in with the little fish. When she came back, the little fish was gone.

"It is not good to do that," said Rosa. "I put the little fish in a bowl so it would be safe."

A. Exercising Your Skill

Read the story. Then answer these questions.

1. What did Emily put into the water?

2. What was in the water already?

3. When Emily came back to look, how many fish were in the water?

4. What did Rosa say was not good to do?

5. What happened to the little fish?

B. Expanding Your Skill

Read these sentences. They tell about the story. Which sentence does not belong?

Emily had a big fish.

Emily put it in the water with the little fish.

The fish became friends.

Rosa put the little fish in a different bowl.

What clues in the story helped you figure out what happened?

C. Exploring Language

What animal does each group of sentences tell about?

1. I live in a large bowl of water. The children look at me. Each day one child gets to feed me. I am bright orange, and I love to swim all day.

   I am a ___.

2. I live in a nice warm house and sleep on a child's bed at night. I have four legs and a tail. My owner shouts at me when I bark or jump up on people. When I am good, I get a bone!

   I am a ___.

3. I live in a zoo. I am a tall animal with a long neck. I love to eat snacks from the tops of trees.

   I am a ___.

D. Expressing Yourself

In a small group, play "Who Am I?" Tell about an animal. Do not name it. See if your friends can name the animal.

The cat saw a balloon. It began to play with the balloon. The cat played too hard! Bam! Where was the balloon? It was gone. The cat did not know what to think.

From the story you can tell that

    (A) the cat did not know the balloon had popped.

    (B) the cat was ready to eat the balloon.

    (C) the cat got another balloon.

The children found a cage. "What will we put in it?" they asked. "It is too big for a fly. It is too small for a deer."

"It is just right for this hamster," said Michael.

From the story you can tell that

(A) the cage was very big.

(B) the deer was too small.

(C) the hamster was put in the cage.

"We can sing something," said Jack. The children began to sing. Then they stopped. They heard funny sounds! What were they?

Then Toni said, "It is just King. He likes to sing too!"

From the story you can tell that

(A) King does not like to sing.

(B) King does not like the children to sing.

(C) at first the children did not know that King was singing too.

"Coach made us swim a mile today," said Nate and Dan. "Swimming makes us hungry."

"You two need to swim well," said Kinu and Emma. "We will cheer for you at the meet tomorrow."

From the story you can tell that

    (A) Nate and Dan are on the swim team.

    (B) Kinu and Emma do not like food.

    (C) Nate and Dan cannot swim.

Chaz watched Mrs. Collins water her flowers. "Why do you water them every day?" he asked.

"The water helps them grow and look pretty," she said.

From the story you can tell that

    (A) Mrs. Collins likes her flowers.

    (B) Chaz is watering the flowers.

    (C) Mrs. Collins does not like her flowers.

The birds made their home. They made it by the window. Luna saw them. What was the home for? Then one day she found out. Baby birds were in it!

From the story you can tell that

    (A) the baby birds did not surprise Luna.

    (B) Luna did not see the birds build the home.

    (C) the baby birds did not build the home.

Ethan was lost in the dark. He took a step. His shoes got wet. Ethan said, "I am near the pond. I will go up where it is dry. I can see the lights from my house up there."

From the story you can tell that

    (A) Ethan wanted to fish.

    (B) Ethan found out where he was.

    (C) Ethan ran for help.

The children saw the acrobats in the air. They held on to their bars and flipped. One even caught the other as he flew from his bar. "They must be very strong," Corey said. "It takes strong muscles to do that trick."

From the story you can tell that

    (A) the acrobats practiced together.

    (B) the children are strong.

    (C) Corey does not like to flip.

The man took a look at all the pigs. Then he saw Kimi's pig. It was a big one. "Your pig is better than the others," said the man. "You win first prize!"

From the story you can tell that

(A) Kimi lost her pig.

(B) Kimi did not really own the pig.

(C) the man had seen other pigs.

Drew found a toy truck. It was still good, but it was old. "Maybe we can make it look new," said Mr. Ellis. Mr. Ellis got some paint. Soon the truck did look like new. Drew was happy.

From the story you can tell that

    (A) the truck was new.

    (B) Mr. Ellis made the truck look old.

    (C) something old can be made to look new.

Alex could not find Tip. "My dog must be lost!" said Alex. She went to her room to cry. She heard a sound under her bed. It was Tip. The dog had been there the entire time!

From the story you can tell that

(A) Alex was sad when she could not find Tip.

(B) Mom saw Tip.

(C) Alex and Tip were lost.

Mrs. Parks came to visit the class. She told a funny story. The children laughed and laughed. Then they picked some flowers for Mrs. Parks. "Thank you for the funny story," the children said.

From the story you can tell that

(A) the boys and girls liked the story.

(B) Mrs. Parks did not like the children.

(C) the story was sad.

Ethan was lost in the dark. He took a step. His shoes got wet. Ethan said, "I am near the pond. I will go up where it is dry. I can see the lights from my house up there."

A. Exercising Your Skill

Read the story above. Tell what Ethan did in the story. Tell the answer to the question below.

ETHAN WAS LOST. What Did Ethan Do?

_____

_____

_____

B. Expanding Your Skill

Talk about the story.

1. Did Ethan know where he was?
2. What happened to his feet?
3. How did Ethan know he was near the pond?
4. What did Ethan think to do?
5. Why was he happy to see the lights of his house?

C. Exploring Language

Think about the following places you could be. Tell what places the sentences are talking about.

1. You are hot. The sun is shining. You cannot wait to jump into the water.
   Where are you?
2. You put the food into the cart. You get in line. You get out your money.
   Where are you?

D. Expressing Yourself

Do one of these things.

1. Read the story in Part A again. Tell a new ending for the story. Draw a picture to go with the story.

2. Have you ever been scared? Tell about a scary thing that happened. The story can be made up, or it can be real.

3. Pretend you are Ethan. Tell your class what you did and how you felt the night you got lost.